Talk of the Town

Warragul/Drouin

Jim Connelly

Other books by Jim Connelly

Tom and Anna on the Trail: the Case of the Missing Schoolgirl

Tom and Anna in Danger: the Case of the Disappearing Dogs

Tom and Anna take a Chance: the Case of the Bungling Bird Bandits

My Folk: Four Hundred Years of Hazards, Tooths, and Connellys

Mountain Boy

Talk of the Town

Warragul/Drouin

Copyright

A CIP catalogue record for this book is available from the National Library of Australia.

First published in Australia 2017

James Timothy Connelly

10 Stoddarts Road

Warragul Victoria 3820.

ajcon@dcsi.net.au

For Mark Biggs, partner in the game of words

Cover photographs by Bev Pascoe

Cover design by aussiepics

Not that the story need be long, but it will take a long while to make it short.

(Henry David Thoreau, 1857)

Warragul Town

One of the best things about Warragul is its shape. You can hold it sideways and you've got these wavy up-hill and down-hill contours. You can look down on it and it puffs out equally in all directions like a nice bulgy cauliflower from Lean and Green. There's a nice balance between the two sides of the railway line, north and south. And above all, the streets go in interesting lines. Some towns go in straight lines, like in Melbourne. Some towns have streets that straggle all over the place, like Sydney. But Warragul has a bit of both. The two main streets start together and grow apart, like twins that have quarrelled. There's another street, nicely bendy, that hooks them together in just the right way. And you've got an arcade in case the weather's stormy. You can even walk through some of the shops and come out the other side, and nobody minds. The Library's up on the hill, where it should be. The Arts Centre, fittingly, is on the edge. The railway station is where the train lines are, which is very convenient. And the hospital is far enough away not to think of it unless we have to, and close enough if we need to it. And the Shire Council building. Where is that? I must ring up and find out.

The Drouin Road

I think the time's coming when Warragul and Drouin will become one great mega town. Economic development will bring it about. Like Albury and Wodonga. Look at the traffic going in each direction. Wow! It's bumper to bumper at school times and nearly as bad at other times. We've even got a morning peak and an evening peak, like in the city. I suppose with all these new houses, you have to get a lot more traffic. We were crooked on them when they put that big roundabout in, but now we can see why. Thank goodness for the 80 kph speed limit, though it seems a suggestion rather than a rule for most drivers. How things have changed. I remember driving that road in the old days when it was the Princes Highway. You'd wave to the driver when you met another car. Now it's all go. I'm amused how at the Lardner's Track traffic lights, when you're coming towards Warragul, some cars change lanes. They get into the left hand lane so they can burn away when the lights go green and get in front of the car that was in front of them. 'City drivers!' I mutter to myself. Then in the middle of it all you see a train gliding past. Maybe that's the way to go. Let someone else have the worry.

A Question of Cats

I haven't noticed too many cats around the streets of Warragul. Dogs, yes; cats, no. The cats are all at home making trouble. The cats round us give us much trouble. They work as a team. They parade through our garden as if they owned it; they perform their toilette in the far corner; they thump on the roof at six o'clock in the morning; they eat our birds. We've thrown things, we've used bad language, we've even tried spraying them with vinegar from a water pistol. They smile and come back the next day. Our fury hath known no limit. How is it we can forgive dogs when they get into mischief, but not cats? Despite all this, we haven't complained. Good neighbourliness, and all that. And so it was until this morning. We'd noticed the grey cat strangely absent for some time. Now we know why. There was a meow this morning. A cute little, soft little meow, and there was a bundle of grey fluffy kittenhood pawing at the fly wire, wanting to come in. Actually wanting to come in! To the house! Our house! What could we do? Admit this representative of evil, or admit that our hearts were stolen? We've lost all our certainties. The future is grey!

Cemeteries

I took a walk through the cemetery the other day. I like cemeteries. You see the names of the men and women who moulded and fashioned and planned, as someone more famous than I once said. Or I suppose some of them did. Probably many of the old-timers just loafed around, while others did the work, just like today. But everyone's different. The cemeteries round here all have great views. It's a happy thought that our forebears are resting in some of the best real estate in town, though, with these developers prowling around, you never know! It's sad to see the little children's graves, and I can't help being sorry for the people whose graves aren't marked at all. I wonder if they wanted it like that or whether they were just too poor for a gravestone. We ought to remember the people on our cemetery trusts who keep the places looking so good. And how do you choose a cemetery if you need one? Do you go for the views from Gulwarra, the tidy grounds of Drouin, the panorama of Trafalgar, or the magpie song of Neerim? Personally, my choice would be for Erica, hidden deep amongst its gum trees. But it's a sunny day today. I'll think about it tomorrow.

Coming into Drouin

You know when you're coming into Drouin, from Warragul I mean, just before that Big Dipper, there's a street on your right. It's called Calway Street and if you go down there, there's a little pocket of nice streets to live in. That's one of the things I like about Drouin. It's got these little places hidden away that a lot of people don't know about. There's another one on the other side of the line. You go over the railway bridge, turn left and you come to a lake with a park and beautiful big gum trees. They call it Goudie Park, and you hardly ever see anyone there. Why not? It's one of the prettiest places for miles. Somebody told me about Mr Goudie. He was Shire President three times and did a lot for Drouin. Another attractive part of Drouin is down where Bellbird Park is. Noisy on Saturday mornings, with all the sport, but a lot of people like the sound of young people. And Flaxmill Close – that's a lovely street. And very historic because of the flax mill that used to be there in the old days. I live near a school, and we hear the sound of kids playing. We love to hear them. Then the bell goes and everything goes quiet. I guess we live in a pretty nice pocket of town, too.

Markets

The first time I saw it, I thought there must have been a revolution or an evacuation. I was driving through Rokeby and found all these cars. Hundreds of them. All over the park and you could hardly get along the road. It was the monthly market! The idea is spreading all over the place. Now there's a market in Drouin and Warragul and Longwarry and Bunyip and Jindivick and Yarragon and Trafalgar. Anywhere else? They arrange them on different weekends, except for Drouin and Warragul. They're on the same day. How did that happen? I go all the time. Mostly to talk to people. I think that's why most people go. But you can buy things as well. There's a lot of organic stuff, and people sell things they've made. I like that. You can make something in your backyard or your kitchen, get a stall, and sell it. Grassroots commerce, they call it. I like to watch the people. A lot walk past the stalls, not going up close in case they get trapped into buying something, but having a good look just the same, out of the corner of their eye. The people selling stuff seem to be enjoying themselves just as much as the punters. Just goes to show. You can have your cake and eat it too.

Cars

Just look around when you're in town. Cars everywhere. They dominate our lives. Think of the roads we build. The petrol stations. The garages. The car yards. The accidents. The registration. Take away the cars and our lives would be empty. What would we talk about? 'How's the Toyota goin', Bluey?' 'Needs a grease and oil, mate. How's ya new blitzer?' If we didn't have cars, President Kennedy would still be alive. What about the Popemobile? He'd need something else to ride in. We live in a car tyranny. A motorocracy. I knew a young couple, well, they were young then, who didn't buy a car. They used taxis instead. Saved a packet. When they retired, they bought a car and went all over the country. Had a ball. The world is divided into two classes of people. Motorists and pedestrians. I'm on the side of the pedestrians, bigtime. Try to cross the road. I was trying to get across Queen Street in Warragul the other day. I started and backed off over and over again. Then I nearly got hit by a car turning left. Without indicating. It's the same in Drouin. Try to cross the main street. You take your life in your hands. Not yours, actually. The hands on that steering wheel.

Street Lights

We mostly take the street lights for granted, but there's a street in Drouin where the people said, 'No thanks, we don't want any street lights.' Well, most of them said that. So now they're in the dark. They said they wanted to see the stars. They didn't want street lights shining in their windows. They wanted to look out and see the darkness. I like the darkness. I always have. For one thing, you can't get sunburnt at night. But I did walk head on into a fence post on a dark night when I was a kid on the farm. I saw lights then, though they weren't street lights. I like the stars, too. I think of the old Australians who made up tales about the stars, and brought the stars into their spirit world. The sailors in the really olden times used to navigate across the oceans using the stars. We've even got some of the stars on our flag. I went on a ship to England once. Each night I went out on the deck and watched the Southern Cross get lower and lower until it vanished altogether. Didn't see it for another year. So I can get alongside those people who wanted to ban the street lights and see the stars. But where I live, it gets pretty dark and dirty on a bad night. I'm happy about the street lights then.

The Railway Station

Railway stations are romantic places. Not mushy romantic. The tug-at-your-heart romantic. Take the Warragul railway station. Some people remember the days of steam, when the Noojee timber train, say, was firing up, or the potatoes were loading and the boss was swearing and the men were sweating, or when the Gippslander pulled into Warragul and the people would rush for the refreshment room for a sandwich and cup of tea. Ten minutes, then they'd be off again. I talked to one of the women who served in that refreshment room. She spoke of those days with tears in her eyes. Now they've restored the place. It's one of Warragul's most beautiful buildings. You should go and see it, though they do keep it locked most of the time. I was catching an early train not so long ago. It was dark and cold. But these people have got a coffee stall there, warm and cosy. The aroma of that brewed coffee was almost worth the price of the train ticket. Then there's the waiting room. Those chaps at the ticket window. Where do they get them from? They take the cake for friendly service. There's a lot going for our railway station. Get down there. It's worth a myki, by crikey.

The Strzeleckis

Have you noticed that the sun always shines on the Strzeleckis? Well, it seems to. I can see the Strzeleckis from my place. On rainy days, we're always looking out and there's the sun shining on the Strzeleckis. People haven't woken up to it; otherwise they'd all be building their houses there. I've seen the Strzeleckis covered with snow, too. Mount Worth was sticking out from the whiteness. There are some hills you can see from all over the place, and Mount Worth is one of them. Wherever you go, you can see Mount Worth. Once those hills were covered with trees. One was so tall they thought it might be a world record, so they chopped it down. You can go there now. There's a plaque to record the fact. Seems a funny thing to do, chop that tree down. They could have used trigonometry to work it out, couldn't they? It's a pity they didn't leave more of those big trees. But I don't suppose they had much time for sentiment, those old fellers. Just wanted some grass for the cows. Now we think all the time about the environment. The trouble is you can't measure the environment in dollars and cents. But we've still got Mount Worth. They can't take that away.

Christmas Day

I drove out to Nilma last year to see the Christmas lights, and found myself in a traffic jam. Wow! The show people put on these days. Crowds come each year. The Shire actually organises tours. You can go to Drouin or Neerim South or Warragul, or just about anywhere, and it's the same. It must look great from space! It was simpler in the old days. Where do you get a threepenny bit to put in the Christmas pudding now? Do the kids still have an orange at the bottom of their stocking? Does Aunty Mary still send her Christmas parcel through the post? My mother had a thing about helping other people at Christmas time. I spent one Christmas Day pulling carrots on a neighbour's place because they hadn't been able to get their crop in, and they depended on it. I'm glad we've gone past that sort of close-to-the-line existence, or we have pretty much. Does that sort of help go on? You could say the Christmas Dinner they put on at one of the churches in Warragul takes up that challenge. They invite everybody who's on their own at Christmas. I was there one year. The Hall was full. Everyone was full of peace and goodwill. 'The Festive Spirit' hardly seems the right name for it.

Anzac Day

I've always felt guilty about not going to the Dawn Service, so I decided to go last year. It was very moving in the semi-darkness, just like when they were landing at Gallipoli, and with the silence, the flames, and the words of the Ode, then the emotion of the Last Post and Reveille. No wonder more and more people are attending these services. At Drouin, there were about the same number as at the main service later in the morning. Hundreds and hundreds. I must go to the early service at the Shrine one day. I've often been to the Shrine, of course. I love that it's built of granite from Tynong, but there's a lot else. There's a book there that lists every person who ever joined up. They turn a page every day. If you ask the man, he'll turn it to where your mother or father or grandfather is listed. Then there's the way they get the sun's rays shining on the words engraved on the floor of the sanctuary exactly at eleven o'clock on the twenty-fifth of April – *'Greater love hath no man'*. It's all pretty spine-tingling. It's good for all of us – especially the kids – to understand what others have done for us. It should help us to be kinder to each other, and that's what those old warriors would want to happen, I should think.

Are You Joking?

They gave the Joke of the Year to this one from Britain: 'I'm not a fan of the new pound coin, but then again, I hate all change.' The simpler the better, I say. My grand-daughter once said, 'There are three kinds of people in the world,' and looked at me expectantly. 'Those who can count and those who can't,' she went on. Then there are the knock-knocks. My five-year-old is just getting into them, and my eight-year-old does nothing but. Like this one. 'Knock knock.' 'Who's there?' 'Boo.' 'Boo who?' 'Stop crying, little baby.' The Gazette has a pile of jokes every Tuesday. I always read them, but then I read anything. People have written PhD theses on jokes. They say there are only a few kinds of jokes in the world – blonde jokes, shaggy-dogs, light-bulb jokes, travelling salesmen jokes, knock-knocks, and Irish jokes (transfer those to any nationality you want). There are puns, sometimes known as 'stop-before-I-scream' jokes. Then there are political jokes. No, I mean actual jokes! Like nominating Barnaby Joyce for New Zealand Citizen of the Year. I'll stop before you scream, but my favourite pun is: Q. 'Is life worth living?' A. 'It all depends on the liver.'

Back Yards

Who owns that lovely red and black ute I saw parked in Drouin the other day? Red front, black back, beautifully painted. About a 1928 model to my untrained eye. I want it! Maybe it's the colours, red and black. Maybe it's that we all hanker after something lovely to look at. Maybe it's the appeal of the past. How many other beautiful old cars are there in our back yards? I meet people all the time who've got an old vehicle they're restoring. And if it's not an old vehicle, it's an old wagon or jinker. Or a rally car. Do they ever finish? I think it's the doing it rather than the finishing it that's more important, like most things in life. Some people grow mushrooms in their sheds. Some have a collection of car number plates. Some have a highly-sophisticated engineering set-up. You can never tell what's there. There should be an annual opening of these places, like the Open Gardens or the Artists-at-Work exhibition days. What interests me is how these back-yard enthusiasts keep it all so quiet. They're the most modest group of people I've ever come across. I'm not like that. If I owned that red and black ute, I'd drive it up and down the main street all day. Every day.

Biggest Morning Tea

I met a man once who didn't have Morning Tea. Strange! Mind you, I allow myself only one morning tea each day. Now they've taken this Morning Tea idea and turned it into a money spinner. I'm not talking about coffee shops. No, it's the Biggest Morning Tea they have each year. Spins money for anti-cancer. You get together, pay your money, drink your tea, and the takings go to Anti-Cancer. They let you have coffee if you want to. It happens in some weird places. The best was when they lined up a hundred people on the trestle bridge at Noojee. Imagine that! How do you get that much hot water in the middle of the bush? Why don't they use the streets? That's what I'd like to see. Get everybody out of all the coffee shops in Warragul (there must be hundreds at any one time), set up tables in, say, Palmerston Street, block off all the traffic, and have a monster Biggest Morning Tea there. They'd curve nicely around the bend. All the coffee shops could combine to serve the tables, and they could take a cut if they wanted to. Then the Warragul Brass Band could serenade the crowd. Come to think of it, why don't they do it every week? That would bring the shoppers back to Warragul.

Bring 'em Up Tough

Kids must have been tougher in the old days. I mean my old days, when I was a child. Take a look at the School Readers that we all had to read. In the Grade 2 book, for six-year-olds, mind you, there's the terrifying story of the hobyahs, who came out at night, creeping through the bush, to eat up the little old man and carry off the little old woman. They are thwarted by yellow dog Dingo until the little old man cuts him into pieces. But there's a happy ending. The dog comes back to life and eats all the hobyahs. What did that story do to our six-year-old minds? Maybe we took it in our stride because we were tougher back then. Or we made out we were! Jump forward to Grade 4. Eight-year-olds. And thrill to the story of the three children, aged nine, seven, and four, lost in the bush for eight days and the agonising account of the search for them. To say nothing of the negative impression of the aborigines: 'Mine tink'it him plenty cry … Him walk slow, slow, slow," says the blacktracker. Perhaps we're too soft these days. Let's give the children stories of murder and animal cruelty and heart-wrenching distress. Maybe we don't need to. It may be all too close to real life for many of them.

Building Boom

There's quite a boom going on. All down the line – Garfield, Bunyip, Longwarry, Drouin, Warragul, Yarragon, Trafalgar – new houses everywhere. You go out looking for mushrooms and you find houses instead. But it's not only houses. Shops, too. In Drouin, there are those new shops at the end of town. A new McDonald's, too. In Bunyip, there's a row of shops just been put in. New churches, as well. In Warragul, there's been a new Uniting Church, a new Salvation Army church, and a new Anglican church in the last few years. In Drouin, there are two new churches. How do they do it? Maybe they charge for admission, like at the pictures. Or do you have to pay to get out? Good luck to them, anyway. Most people like the church to be there, even if they don't go each week. They closed the church in Ellinbank, and the same with the church in Nilma. I guess it's hard to run a church when they're so close to Warragul. People can jump in their cars and be in town in a few minutes. Haven't noticed many new pubs lately. Maybe there's no money in pubs anymore. Everybody must be playing golf or riding bikes or running marathons instead. Or going to church?

Children Playing Games

Sometimes when it's not too hot and not too cold and not too wet and not too windy I go for a walk. I go past one of our State schools, and lo and behold, the other day they were playing hopscotch. Hopscotch! I thought that was a thing of the past, like hypol and lard and a pound of broken biscuits, please. But there they were, these little kids, throwing their bits and hopping down the squares, just like we used to do. We'd scratch the lines in the dirt. It must be hard to find a decent piece of dirt these days, and I suppose that's one reason why the game has gone into a decline, with asphalt and concrete and artificial grass everywhere. These kids had got a piece of chalk to draw their lines. Pinched it from the classroom I suppose. Do they still use chalk these days? The best thing about hopscotch is the arguing. That's true about all kids' games. You argue the toss and twist the rules and make up things to suit yourself. But you're learning how to live with others all the time, and how far you can go. It's a bit like Parliament, only they're worse. Next time you're walking past a school, have a look. They may be playing hopscotch. Or even jacks. Now that's another thing …

Citizenship

I went to a citizenship ceremony in Warragul. There were all these people who wanted to be dinky-di Australians. When my wife was naturalised, she had to promise to defend the Queen and Country against the enemy. You wouldn't want to put her in the front line now, she says. Nowadays they want you to answer a test. A whole lot of questions to show you know something about the country. There's a lot of argy-bargy going on about it. I reckon they should have different tests for different places. Local tests. So, round here they'd ask, 'What was the name of the horse from Labertouche that won the Melbourne Cup?' or Where did Crossover get its name from?' or What's the frequency of the local community radio?' Simple questions like that. You hear a lot of people saying that everyone who comes to Australia should have to learn the language. What language? That's the problem. I say that if they can carry on an ordinary conversation, that's enough, like, 'How ya goin, mate, orright?' 'Good enough to sink a couple. Yaself?' 'Bleedin' good, mate.' Nino Culotta wrote a book about it – 'They're a Weird Mob.' They ought to hand out copies of that.

Coffee Shops

Now I need some advice. Where do I get a good cup of coffee? Drouin or Warragul, either will do. It needs to be hot, that's the main thing. And stay hot. Can they do that? I like flat white, and it cools off so fast I have to drink it quickly and then I feel I haven't got my money's worth. See what I mean? Other people make their coffee last half an hour sometimes while they yakker away, and there's me sitting with an empty cup and feeling out of it. But it's not just the coffee I want to know about. Where's the best place for conversation? For sitting round and putting the world to rights? Like Dr Johnson and his cronies in the good old days. They sat around and drank their coffee and smoked their long-stemmed pipes, and they changed England. Now that's the sort of thing I'm looking for. I'd be the Dr Johnson. I can imagine the scene. We'd have a crowd of people calling out for their coffee, serving wenches in aprons running around with their steaming coffee pots, pipe smoke everywhere, a log fire roaring, and we'd really go to town on the Shire Council, after we'd dealt with Spring Street and Canberra. Where can I find a coffee shop like that? Maybe I'll start my own. Any takers?

Concert Halls

We're getting a fine new Arts Centre. So we should, now we're coming so close to the city. Even more of those Melbourne people will come to see a show. And from the Valley. How about what they did when the Arts Centre was out of action! They put all the shows on in the little country halls. It was somebody's brilliant idea. So we had the Fred Astaire show in the Jindivick Hall. Burt Bacharach went to Darnum. You know, the Darnum Hall, where we used to go to the dances! Another show went to Labertouche, and another to Narracan. Narracan! Up all those twisty roads and back, in the dark. It probably started off as a joke, but it worked. But that's not all. The Crow Family – that's the name of the show – were on at Neerim Junction. Stone the crows! There was a show about the 1940s at Yarragon. That seems appropriate. Shirley Valentine went to Trafalgar. Other things were on at Wesley. Well, we all know Wesley. I went to some of those shows. The performers were right there in front of you. You could almost touch them if you were in the front row. They should keep it going. 'Variety for the Villagers,' they could call it. Or 'Theatre in the Thistles'. I'd give that an encore.

Crossing the Road

I regard myself as a pretty good pedestrian. I once crossed the main square in Cairo in peak hour. They make it easier for pedestrians round here. In Drouin, they make the cars stop for you, and they've even put in flashing lights, though whether they're there to warn the car drivers or the people crossing I'm not too sure. In Warragul, they've raised the crossings in Smith Street, so you can look down your nose at the cars that pull up for you. It's the intersections you have to be careful about. These cars come at you from behind, round the corner, and you have to do a bit of eye-contact negotiating with the driver, but it's all in the game, as Nat King Cole once said. There's another tricky place in Victoria Street, where you're trying to get across to Harvey Norman, and they've made a place that looks like a pedestrian crossing, but they haven't put in any white stripes, so the cars get first go. The safest place to cross the road is Neerim South. The cars only go one way, and there are so few of them it makes it easy, though it takes away from the sport. Isn't it funny, though, how when you cross the street and get in your car, everything changes. Get out of my way, you crazy ********.

Early Morning Walk

Just back from my early morning walk. We'd run out of milk. Thank goodness for corner shops. We'll have to get some of that long-life stuff. They say you can keep it for months. Now, my walk. It was COLD! Ah! Bitter chill it was. The hare limped trembling through the frozen grass. Well, I didn't actually see any hares, but that line of poetry is what it felt like. Frost on the grass there was, and sun on my back, so I was feeling pretty good. Not many people about, but birds everywhere. One magpie stood there on the ground not two feet away and didn't move as I walked past. Probably mistook me for St Francis. I could hear the crows in the trees. Ravens, someone told me they were, not crows, but they seem the same to me No corellas, though. Too early in the morning. They sleep in till the sun warms the place up, then they have a great corroboree flying around and screeching their war songs. Then, on the last bit, downhill now, I met these three runners. Two girls and a bloke. The chap was lagging behind, but they were all talking and laughing. Now how do you do that? Run – uphill - and laugh, all at the same time. I bet George W Bush couldn't do that.

Eating Out

You'd wonder if anyone was at home, with all the people eating out. If you put together the clubs and the restaurants and the hotel dining rooms and the fast food outlets, you'd have about a thousand people dining out on average each night. That's in Warragul alone. It's true. I've done the sums. That's one in twelve of Warragul's population. Or, to put it another way, each person in Warragul dines out every twelfth night. Perhaps that where Shakespeare got the idea! I can understand why there's all this dining out. It's because the tucker's so good. I hope the people who cook at home aren't offended! But whenever I eat out, the food's always terrific. I've got one favourite place that I can't mention because I've got friends elsewhere, too. We took our sophisticated city offspring there. They were inclined to be a little supercilious beforehand, but they came away saying it was better than they've come across in the big smoke. From them, that's a big recommendation! I'm still getting used to some of the modern trends, though. I don't like paying extra for the 'sides', and why do they hide the vegies under the meat? Nevertheless, I'd give them all five stars any day.

Emergency Department

I'm reporting from the front line. I was wounded yesterday, and my wife decided I should go to the field hospital, otherwise known as the emergency department of the hospital. They've got a really good system there. A nurse works out the general gist of the problem at the front window, and when they see you're not going to expire immediately, they get you to wait in the superbly-named Waiting Room. They were showing the North Melbourne-St Kilda match on the telly. I looked for the meat pie stall, but that was one of the fail points of the service. There wasn't one. Then you go in to one of those cubicles. Each one has got enough gear in it for a heart transplant, should they need it. One doctor sees you and works out what to do, then another doctor comes along and does it. They give you quite a lot of time to lie there and enjoy yourself. They all seem to know each other pretty well. There was a lot of laughing and chyacking amongst all the doctors and nurses and cleaners and the ambulance drivers who wandered in. There was a camera up in the corner. I'm not sure whether they were recording everything or filming the next episode of Hospital-Five-O. Must watch and see.

Ficifolias

Some people say you should pronounce the word, 'Fick-a-folia'. But it sounds much better the other way, the way we all pronounce it. A lot of people think ficifolias have always grown in Drouin. But they actually come from round Albany in Western Australia. That's where they all started. I've been learning a lot about ficifolias. They've taken them to New Zealand. There's one ficifolia over there that's more than two metres in diameter. You'd need three people to join hands to get around it. Most ficifolias do their best every second year. Did you know that? Drouin's famous for its ficifolias. They're everywhere. Some were planted by the State School kids years ago. The Ficifolia Festival in Drouin is one of the best shows in the district. Probably the best. They put it on in February when the trees are flowering, and they run all sorts of events – art shows, talks, displays, poetry and plays, open days, and kick it all with a big dinner. People put scarecrows in their front gardens one year. On the last day, there's a parade through the main street that anyone can go in. Thousands go to watch it. My mate and I are thinking of going in it, dressed as Bill and Ben, the flower-pot men.

Football Teams

I see Drouin want to go back to the West Gippsland Football League, where they used to be, playing against Longwarry and Bunyip and teams like that. I remember the old days in that league, when the de Vries boys were playing, but I don't expect many will remember that. Then they put Drouin in with Traralgon and Sale, and we thought, 'How can they do that? – Drouin against those big places.' But then you think of Maffra, who do so well in the big league. Anyway, Drouin did all right for themselves most of the time. I see they call these clubs 'Football-Netball clubs' these days. I suppose it's all about the girls getting their recognition. Each club has to have its netball teams as well. And they've got women's football, too. You have to say it's all right, unless you're a head-in-the-sand ostrich. I went to the Warragul-Drouin match last time they played. It was like the way they play in Melbourne – all handball and play-on and don't worry about your man stuff. I wonder what would happen if they went back to how we used to play. Stick on your man, kick the ball - towards your own goal, not the opposition's. You never know. You might lose by even more!

Fun Run

They have this Fun Run in Warragul each year. The Shire and the Gazette both have a hand in it, and a lot of businesses and clubs put money into it, too. Kathy Watt organises it, and it's held in memory of her father. The Watts have been a notable sports family. Every town needs some people to look up to, and the Watts do that for Warragul, amongst a lot of others. I've given up running myself. If I did have a go, it would be an UnFun Run for me. I just go and have a geek. Some folk do five-kilometres and others the half-marathon., but you can run other distances, too, if you like. You should have a go yourself. Some people wear fancy dress. Some take their dog. You can push your baby in a pusher if you like. As one of my friends would say, 'It's a hoot!' You can register on the web. You pay a bit of money, of course. Nobody cares about winning, or hardly anybody. Some of the top runners from Melbourne and other places come, and there was one of those classy Africans one year. I suppose they're trying to win. But don't let that worry you. I nearly forgot to say. They have a free barbecue after it's finished. I wonder if it's for onlookers like me, as well!

Funeral

I went to a funeral the other day. A minister took it, but it was in the Funeral Chapel. I don't know why they do that. I suppose they hadn't been to church for a while and they thought they shouldn't just pop up at the end and ask for a service in the church. Anyway, it was a good service. This woman had done a lot of good things, and she'd had a difficult time towards the end. You couldn't help feeling she was a lot better off, and that's what her children said, when they spoke. At the wake afterwards, it's a funny thing, but you think you should be talking about the person who's died, but everyone talks about the weather and the football and how crook they are. At the end of the service the minister said something I liked. He said it summed up this woman's life. It was a poem:

Life is mostly froth and bubble/ Two things stand like stone

Kindness in another's trouble/ Courage in your own.

Sounds like a pretty good way to live. And now I remember where I've heard it before. It was in one of the old State School readers. Remember them?

Furry Friends

'*Adopt a furry friend,*' the notice said. The Shire Council's notice in the Gazette. '*Visit the Lost Animals Register to see what cuddly creatures are available for adoption,*' it went on to say. '*They're looking for a new loving home right now*'. That sounded good to me. I spoke to my wife. She agreed. 'We could find something for our grand-daughter as well.' We were glowing with anticipation. So I went on the Shire website and clicked through to the Lost Animals Register. There were three ginger cats to begin with. 'Mmm,' we said. 'Let's look further.' Next came a staghound. Maybe a little large. Next were two more cats and a kelpie. "People are very careless with their animals,' I said to my wife. But then came the climax. '*Three Friesian cows. Found at Rokeby.*' We scratched our heads. 'Help with the lawn-mowing,' my wife suggested. "Do we have to take all three?' I wondered. 'Maybe two for the grand-daughter and one for us" my wife said. 'Cuddly creatures?' I said. 'Furry friends?' my wife replied. There was a photo. 'They look very nice,' muttered my wife. I put my foot down. 'No Friesians!' I declared. 'Jerseys?' my wife responded. 'They're lovely.'

Garbage Bins

Friday. Bin night. Our recyclable bin is always full. We call it 'Osama'. You know – Osama bin laden. Why is it that the garbage bins are the cause of so much domestic strife? People argue about them all the time. I've got a mate who went to a backyard wedding here in town, and he swears that when the bridegroom made his vows he swore he would put out the bins each week. It's bringing them in again that bothers me. The record in our street is bringing the bins in the day before they had to go out again. Although that same mate tells me he knows of one place where they kept the bins out the front all the time and took the rubbish out to them when they needed to. Maybe the Shire could give an award for the 'Best Bins Street.' Make it monthly, and no street can win it twice running. Or would it be better to name and shame? Make it a 'Worst Bins Street'. I'd volunteer as the judge. And spare a thought for the truck drivers. I know one bloke who goes out when he hears the truck coming and passes up a jar of home-made jam to the driver every now and then. Then the driver picks up his bin and puts it down right in front of him. That's a good way to make friends.

Gippsland Cheese

I was speaking to someone up in Queensland and I mentioned that I was from Gippsland. They said, 'Gippsland! Where all the good cheese comes from!' Well, it was good to hear that. We always like to hear good things about where we come from. Our local cheese has won prizes all round the world. I wonder why Gippsland makes such good cheese. Maybe it's the grass. Maybe it's the contented cows. Probably it's the skill of the cheesemakers more than anything. I tried to make cheese once. At home, in the kitchen. I got some fresh milk straight from the cow. That's not hard to do round here. I put some vinegar into it, covered it over, and left it keeping warm. After a while, I poured off the liquid. Strained it all through a piece of cloth. It was an iridescent green colour, but you don't worry about that. I hung it up to drip out and go solid, then I shaped it up and put it on the table. There was some salt in there somewhere, as well. It wasn't too bad, but as George Calombaris would say, I've tasted better. Still, I haven't tried it again, and that says something! Why don't you have a go? If it doesn't work, you can slip down to the shop and pick up a piece of Gippsland Blue.

Glen Cromie

I was out at Glen Cromie not long ago, at Drouin West. The Tarago River flows through it. Very pretty. It was burnt out in the 2009 bushfire, but you don't see much of that now. There were aboriginal people out there thousands of years ago. You don't see much of them there now, either, but if you stop and think about it, it makes us look pretty much like new chums. How would it be to walk around the place and know that your father's father and all your fathers ad infinitum walked here just like you? That's how it is for our aboriginal people. But that's not all. The land and the birds and the animals and the clouds: they're all part of them, somehow. And they feel part of it. It's a bit mysterious, but that's how it is. I can't really understand it. I can get it in my brain but not in my mind. You'd reckon the aboriginal folk would think of us as newcomers or intruders, but if they do, they don't say it out loud. They're very gentle people. I only met Lionel Rose once, but I saw that film about him. He was a very gentle fellow, very forgiving. Like the others. You can see the past in them. We should think more about the past, it seems to me. It might help us get through our future.

Going Down the Street

I could walk down the street, but it's a bit far. So I mostly take the car. I should get the old bike out, I suppose. I've got one down in the shed. I've done it a couple of times – ridden the bike - but one of the things that put me off was all the broken glass in the bike lane. You'd be amazed what people do – have a bingle or break a bottle, then sweep all the junk where the bikes have to go over it. They call it a bike lane, but then they let the cars park there as well. So you're riding your bike along and dodging out in front of the traffic every time you come to a parked car. Rather like the dodgem cars! But there's another way of getting into town people are talking about. All these new buses. Well, they've always been there, but they've jazzed up the timetable, so all these shiny buses are darting about all over the place, in Drouin and Warragul, at any rate. I actually saw two people waiting at a bus stop the other day. Getting more like the city every day! And someone told me they caught the bus to the railway station, then the train to Pakenham, and came back home the same way. Left the car in the garage. Said something about saving the planet. Might be worth a try.

Going to the Flicks

We went to the pictures last night. Up the stairs, buy some popcorn, through the drafting race, pick up the tickets. It's the routine that grabs us. Along the corridor, and into the theatre, then the whispered quarrel about where to sit. 'No, we'll be in front of them'. 'Let's go over the other side'. Sit a bit along from the couple behind, a bit the other way from the couple in front. Count the people. Ten. No, a man arrives. How can they make a quid out of eleven people? Then the ads start. Nearly breaks your eardrum to begin with. Then the film. No, it's a trailer. Here it is. No, another trailer. 'Well, we won't come to that.' 'These trailers put you off, if you ask me.' At last. It starts. Eleven people wrapped together in silence for a hundred and twenty minutes. Strange! But there's a real sense of camaraderie. How would you get on with these people in broad daylight if they put you together for two hours with only yourselves there, and you have to talk to each other? Now, the film's over. People rush to get away as if the prison door is thrown open. We sit until all the credits roll through. Trying to get our full money's worth, I suppose. Outside, peanuts and lollies, cries the boy downstairs.

Graffiti Artists

Here's a question. What's the difference between a street artist and a graffiti bandit? Please write and tell me. I went to that lane in Melbourne famous for its wall painting. Just off Flinders Street. 'So this is what makes Melbourne the world's most liveable city' I muttered. And why is it graffiti artists have such a fixation with transport – train carriages, railway bridges, buses? Things may not be so bad down our way. But the tags – see how I've researched the subject! – are so pathetic I feel sorry for the kids who've done them. Assuming they are kids. That's a thought. Maybe they're done by the Senior Citizens on a moonlit night. Graffiti was once an art, and what was written was poetic or philosophical. At Pompeii someone wrote, 'If you ignore a problem, it will only get bigger.' Someone else, 'Lovers are like bees; they live a honeyed life.' That was in 79AD! Our first people had no words to write, but they drew incredible pictures on cave walls, pictures that are messages, too. That's real art. But I mustn't complain too much. These graffiti artists grow out of it, I'm told. And there's always the chance to do a bit ourselves. I'd recommend using white paint – on a white wall!

Horses in the Street

Wonder of wonders! In Drouin this week I saw someone riding a horse down the street. There was a time we'd hear the clip-clop of hooves in the street all the time. Well, pad-pad, I suppose, because they were dirt roads back then. There were more blacksmiths than garages. There were even drinking troughs for the horses at the side of the road. The butcher would come round with his horse and cart. Called at each house in the street. Same with the baker. With the milkman we'd leave a jug at the front door, and he'd fill it up from the can at the back of his cart. No one worried about germs back then. Perhaps we should have! The smart ones would wait for the horse to do his thing; then they'd duck out with a bucket and spade and pick it up for their tomatoes. There was the Indian trader, as well. He had his horse and cart, though the Rawleighs man always seemed to have a van. In the really old days, the kids would ride their horses to school. Each school had to have a paddock for the horses. Can't see it happening today. The poor old horse. I'm afraid he's had his day. Except for one thing. There's always the first Tuesday in November! The nation stops for a horse race!

Houses for Sale

Wow! I wouldn't like to be a house at the moment. They'd have me up for sale in the blink of an eye. Everywhere you go in Drouin you see the signs up, and it's the same in Warragul. There was once the time when we bonded with our house. We had a kind of loyalty to it. We belonged to the house as much as the house belonged to us. Now people sell their house before they really get to know it. How can they sell so many houses, we're all asking. Where are the people coming from? And people must be leaving. Where are they going? That's another mystery. It's hard to get to know people when there's this turnover. I spoke to one fellow last week, and today there's a furniture van outside his house. And all these new houses they're building. They're so big they'll cost the earth when they eventually come up for sale. How will young people afford them? But then, on the other hand, someone was telling me, they might cost more, but at least they don't cost so much to live in as the old ones because they have a lot of energy-saving tricks built into them. Well, most of them. And I see a lot of solar panels going on to roofs lately. Good to see that. Power on a hot tin roof!

How's your Hearing?

They say men don't go to the doctor as often as they should. Nor to the audiologist. I never thought I'd have any trouble with hearing. I've always known my hearing was perfect. Though it's strange, I thought, how women's voices change over the years. Take my wife. She used to have a clear strong voice. It's getting softer lately. Often I have to ask her to speak louder. 'Could you turn to face me when you're speaking,' I've had to ask. She always replies with some caustic comment about it's me, not her. We carried on for a long time, as married couples do, in this state of mutual misunderstanding. About that time we went on holidays to Queensland. There was a stall there in a shopping mall, saying '*Free hearing tests.*' Well, I can't walk past a free offer at any time, so I stepped up to the plate, grinning superciliously. Five minutes later, it was the test lady doing the grinning. 'Severe loss in the higher register,' she said. Well, I couldn't take that lying down. I went to a place in Warragul to get the right diagnosis. Same result. 'We have very discreet hearing aids these days,' the man said. So far I've rejected his advances, but I feel I'm on the losing side in this one.

In the Dark

I did much of my growing up sitting in the picture theatre on Saturday nights. Where else could I learn? No-one was telling me about the important things in life, like bravery against the odds, and whipping the Indians, and love. Especially love. What was this thing everyone talked about? I was six years old, remember. It seemed to my poor understanding that it must be a physical thing and that when it struck I would be irrevocably changed. You *fell* in love. Love is *blue*. Love *never ends*, they told us. I had a very practical mind. How could I put all this together? Then, one happy night, I received words of comfort from the silver screen. The young man was talking to the wise old guy, and asked him, 'How can I tell if I'm in love?' and the answer came directed in a manner unexpected: 'You will know. When it happens you will know. There will be no doubt.' It seems somewhat insubstantial from my present vantage point, but I was satisfied. I could wait without anxiety. I would know when the time came. So I settled into a peaceful state of relaxation. Until – here's the rub – I fell in love. The next year. When I was seven. It was true love. I knew. There was no doubt.

Knitting

Some folks like to do some things and other folks like to do other things. Some people build model train tracks; some collect teaspoons; and some like to knit. It's mostly women who like to knit, but not all. There was a boy at school who was a whizz at knitting, and I, also, learnt the art. I could do plain, but struggled with purl, and someone had to cast on for me. I don't think I ever finished anything. I can watch others knitting for hours. Like I can watch trains shunting or balers baling. With knitting, it's not just the mechanics of using the needles. It's the sheer wonderment of someone picking up those two needles, taking a hank of wool, and making something useful out of it. How does all that stuff hang together? There's deep physics in there. You can't even rip it apart. And knitting promotes conversation. Have you ever noticed that? Take two people, or more, put them together with knitting needles in their hands, and the chance of them being silent is about the same as a Collingwood supporter not complaining about the umpire. I think I'll go back to knitting. It will be good for me. I'll sit and knit, or maybe I'll just sit and think of other days when I sat and knat.

Letter from the Queen

There's a chap I've got to know. Lives round the corner and down the hill a bit. I see him in his garden when I walk past. He turned ninety, he was telling me, and he got a letter from the Prime Minister. How did the Prime Minister know, I asked. Well, it seems that you have to organise it yourself. He told me all about it. You go down to the Federal Member's office in Warragul, or get someone to do it for you, some time beforehand, and show them your birth certificate, and it just happens from there. Not only that. He's going to get a letter on his birthday every year from now on. Seems a bit extravagant to me, but I didn't tell him that. That's not all. I started asking round, and I found you can organise yourself a letter from the Governor-General when you've been married fifty years, and, if you can last that long, the Queen sends you a letter for your sixtieth wedding anniversary or when you turn 100. All done through the Federal Member. I'd have thought he had other things to do, and maybe he has. But with so many people these days living so long, it must take a lot of his time. I wonder about when he turns 100. Would he write a letter to himself?

Linear Trail

You can go for miles along the linear trail in Warragul. It's wonderful. Nice and flat. You meet people. You breathe in the fresh air. You say, 'Ah! Life is beautiful'. There *are* one or two problems. You have to cross the main Drouin Road, though they've put pedestrian lights to help you. Then you cross Bowen Street. No lights there. You have to go through the look-to-the-right, look-to-the-left routine. Then there are the dogs. It must be one of those off-the-leash zones. They come at you as if they hadn't seen anyone for a week. And you say, 'Lovely little dog' to the owner, while all the time you want to say, 'Get out of my way, you little so-and-so'. You needn't bother saying anything to the runners. Not those with headphones. They're in a world of their own. In one place there's this creek running beside you, and you've got to watch out for that. You might slide into it, or that little dog might push you over the edge, if you're on a bike, especially. It's a wonder the Health and Safety people don't do something about it. The best part is where you go under the railway line, and the train goes over you. It brings out the little boy in me. 'Who's that going over my bridge?' said the troll.

Local Papers

I get the Gazette each Tuesday. Can't do without it. I do a quick scan – the front page, the Letters to the Editor, then the deaths, in that order. I read the rest later in the day. We're well off for papers round here. Just take a look next time you're at the newsagent's. There's the Australian, the Herald-Sun, the Age, the Financial Review, the Weekly Times, and then you can get the Pakenham Gazette and the Warragul Citizen as well as the Warragul Gazette. And the Trader on Thursdays, of course. They say that newspapers aren't selling like they used to. Circulations seem to be going down. A lot of people read the paper on-line. Costs less that way, but then you have to sit in front of your computer screen to read it. Or look at your phone, if you have one of those fancy new ones. Wouldn't suit me. I like to have the paper in my hand. I like to make a mess of it before my wife has a chance to. I like to look back at last week's paper to check on something. Then I like the fun of realising you've thrown it away in the recycling. I don't reckon the Gazette will be declining. We need the local gossip, and, as we all know, it's gossip that makes the world go round.

Made in Australia

There's nothing like teamwork. My wife and I believe in teamwork. We've always gone shopping as a team. She's done the shopping and I've unloaded the car when she got home. I used to go with her, but I spent so long comparing the prices per 100 grams it drove her crazy. I looked at the labels when she got home the other day. '*Made in Vietnam*,' it said. On a tin of sardines. 'Why can't you buy Australian sardines?' I cried. 'Because we don't make them,' she replied. Undaunted, I tried again. Tomato paste, this time. '*Product of China*,' it had on it. 'Got you!' I called. 'We've got tons of tomatoes in Australia.' My wife is not one to be easily outpointed. Without a blink, she came up with this: 'If we don't buy from other countries, they won't buy from us. There are trade treaties, and things like that.' This was a severe setback, but I rallied. 'So they buy iron ore from us and we buy tomato paste from them. Gina Rinehart gets rich and our tomato growers go broke.' I could see she was wavering, so I went for the punch-line. 'Dumb sort of trade treaty!' I said. I don't know quite how it happened, but now I go and do the shopping, and my wife stays home and unloads the car. Teamwork!

Mancaves

There's a new word in the English language – mancave. It means a place for the man of the house to escape to, usually a shed in the back yard. Some say it's sexist. It goes back to Dagwood. Remember Dagwood, the comic strip, where Dagwood, the husband, was always being shown up as being dumb by his wife, Blondie. But I've always said each person in a house needs their own special space. It may be a mancave for a man or a craft room for the woman, or the other way round. So I'm in favour of mancaves. They're now making public mancaves. In Warragul, it's the Warragul Woodies. In Drouin it's the Drouin Men's Shed. The Warragul Woodies have their place out at Lillico, which sounds a bit odd, and you can come from other places, like Drouin, if you like. The Drouin Men's Shed is at the Golf Course in Drouin. Some men go there from Warragul! They do great things at both places, making and mending and sharing and laughing. Sounds good. Keeps them off the streets, anyhow! I haven't joined up. My manual skills don't go beyond hanging a picture on the wall. I did Woodwork at school and failed. Nobody fails at the Woodies. Nor the Men's Shed.

Manners

There was a time when a man would stand up when a lady ('woman', if you like) came into the room. I'm told you might get an earful from the lady if you do it now. Women's lib and equality of the sexes and all that. I'm all for women's lib, but I think there's room for some old-fashioned gentility. How about a man always walking on the outside of the footpath? It started in times when the coaches would splash mud from the road, and the man would get his cloak dirty rather than the lady. I still do it. I walk on the outside of the footpath if I'm walking with a woman in the street. And if a lady is coming towards me I go to the outside, the road side. I did this the other day and the woman veered on to the grass to keep away from me. And looked at me in a funny way. I dunno! Do they teach manners to the kids these days? I don't mean at school. They've got enough to do. But at home. I suppose it doesn't matter too much about standing up for a lady or walking on the outside of the footpath. But how about 'Pass the salt, please.' Or 'May I leave the table now?' Or 'Can I help you?' There's an old phrase, 'Manners makyth man'. Now where did that come from?

People in the Street

You know how people say you should park your car some distance from where you're going and walk from there. It does you good, they say. Sometimes I do it. But I do it because that way I meet people. I talk with some of them. A lot, I just nod, and they nod back. I'm thinking, 'Now, who's that?' and they're thinking the same. The trouble starts when one of these people stops and starts talking, and you're thinking like mad, 'Who the dickens is this bloke?' He knows you. He uses your name, and here you are groping for a clue. If the penny does drop, you spend the next five minutes using his name every second sentence, and you go away slapping him on the back and saying he must come round some time. Other times, a pretty girl smiles at you, and you think 'What's going on?' Then you remember it's old Sam's granddaughter. Ah well, life wasn't meant to be exciting. Then there was the time I saw this woman coming towards me. I thought she looked familiar. I don't see all that well these days. She stopped and asked in a familiar tone what I was doing sauntering round the streets. Then I recognised her. We've been married forty years, you know.

Neerim South

I like Neerim South. The name rolls off the tongue, for a start. Try it against some of our other towns and you'll see the point. They've got sculpture in the street, and nobody complains about it. There's a nice bend in the road and one-way traffic. Always plenty of parking. There's only one pub, so you don't get any arguments about where to go for a drink. It's local, yet it's cosmopolitan because of all the snow traffic. And only one football team. In some places you get a lot of argufying between different teams. Not in Neerim South. And the public library is in the school. Now, that's a good idea! It brings the town into the school and the school into the town. Everybody gets to know everybody else. Someone told me they've got a great community walking group. And all around there are these big hills. Or the Tarago, if you look the other way. It's a river. Warragul's only got Hazel Creek. Some towns don't have any creeks or rivers at all. But the best thing about Neerim South is that the mail comes in half-way through the morning, and everybody goes down to get their mail at the same time. You hear all the gossip. Just like the old parish pump.

New Developments

A rose by any other name would smell as sweet, said Shakespeare. Well, I've been noticing the names our new streets are getting. They're not too bad. I believe there's a Committee that sees to that. The same doesn't seem to apply to the housing estates popping up everywhere. The developers must have the right to name their sub-divisions. I think the Shire should control it. They're calling that new development out on the Drouin Road 'Highvale Rise'. Bit syrupy, isn't it? So many of these developments are given 'nothing' names. Take 'Crystal Waters' or 'Chesterfield Heights' or 'Waterford Rise'. And others just like that. All a bit like bananas and custard, don't you think? The next one will be 'Paradise Heights'! It reminds me of the names they give to homes for the aged, not round here, thankfully, like 'Eventide Homes'. Some street names have got a bit of daring in them, like Beckham Court and Cantona Court in Warragul. Some originality there. They should do the same with housing developments. How about some aboriginal names? Or some of our pioneers? Something distinctive rather than chic and fuzzy. A sub-division by any other name would smell as sweet!

No Money

You don't need money these days. You just need a bank account and a credit card. I can go down the street, buy everything I need, and not hand over a cent. I went to the doctor and paid by card. The next morning most of that was back in my bank account. Simply marvellous. It reminds me of the old days. You'd go into a store like Porters in Drouin or Burtons in Warragul. They'd put your money in a little container, pull the cord, and it would shoot up to the cashier who counted it, and returned your change and your receipt in the same container. Then the grinning shop assistant would hand it over to you. That was real money, but it was the same system. I bet the banks don't have any money. I don't mean the local banks like the ones down the street, but the headquarter banks. They do everything on paper or else it's all in their computers. Then they lend money to you. I can't work that out. The banks take money from some people and lend it out to other people. It's not their money; it's other people's. But they charge you interest to have it. How can they do that? The government should look into it. But then they're doing the same, I suppose. It's not their money!

Opportunity Shops

I bought a pair of shoes for eight dollars. Really good ones. I wore them for years, even overseas. I got them from an op shop in Warragul. I won't say which one. I might cause a stampede. Most towns have got op shops these days. They must make a lot of money for the charities that run them. There's one in Drouin that gives away tens of thousands of dollars each year. Others do the same. You should go into one of these places. All these women, mostly, having a ball. Some customers are on the lookout for cheap things because they haven't got much money, and others are just after a bargain. Then they can show their friends and say, 'Look what I bought at the op shop,' and their friends will envy them, and isn't that what we want in life? Some people won't admit they go to op shops. When their friends say, 'Where did you get that?' they say 'Oh, just from a little boutique down the street.' I like to think of the man who wore my shoes before I did. I think he'd be happy that I'm so pleased with them. Thank you, Mister. If you don't want to let on you bought something from the op shop, don't forget to cut the price tag off as soon as you get home. It's a dead giveaway.

Our Days are Numbered

Our days are numbered. There's our tax file number, our bank account number, our credit card number, the computer password number, maybe an ABN number, and, for some of us, six magic numbers that might bring us happiness some sweet Saturday night. There's also a number we each have outside our house. Some put it on their letter boxes, some on their front gate, some paint it on the gutter. We have to have it by law, I was told. So do shopkeepers. How many shopkeepers do you know who have their street number outside their shop? You could count them on the fingers of one hand. The Queen Street ones are the worst, in Warragul. I wanted to buy something the other day. I looked up the pink pages. Well, they used to be pink. There was a shop that sold what I wanted. It was at number a hundred and something in Queen Street. Cheerfully, I set off, keeping a keen look out for the shop numbers from the car window. I couldn't see any! Up and down Queen Street I cruised until I nearly ran out of petrol. Some people talk about looking after Number 1. Not if you're a shopkeeper, it seems to me. Unless you happen to be Number 1 in the street!

Parking

One of the favourite sports in both Drouin and Warragul is to cruise the streets looking for a parking spot. It's a pastime that can get you hooked. You can spend hours at it. The rules are that you drive very slowly round the town, watching the backs of the parked cars. As soon as you see a car's reversing lights go on, you jam hard on the brakes, and wait for the other car to reverse out and drive away. The longer you hold up the car behind you, the more points you get. Sometimes I grab a spot like this, not because I need it – I might be on my way home to lunch – but because of the satisfaction of securing a spot. There's a wonderful feeling of achievement to be gained. There's a growing trend for cars coming in the opposite direction – they're mostly four-wheel-drives, I've noticed - to swing enterprisingly across the white line and grab an empty spot. This is known as 'crab-holing', and earns double points. The spoil-sports have built a barrier down the middle of Smith Street in Warragul to prevent crab-holing. A petition is currently being taken up to have this removed. The purists, however, believe it's not the points you earn, but the way you play the game.

Physical Jerks

Who said young people don't get enough exercise? They should go down to Bellbird Park on a Saturday morning. It's the same in Burke Street, in Warragul. The kids are so thick on the ground it's hard to tell one game from another. They're like ants. I suppose the parents organise it all. It's best to start them young. I know a boy who's four years old. His father took him to Mount Cannibal. They went up it and came down again. Then the kid said, let's do it again, so they did. Straight off. He won't be one of those obese kids you hear about, I'll guarantee. I heard about someone who mixed up 'obese' and 'obtuse'. She complained about all the obtuse children she saw down the street. The kids do PE in school, more than they used to. I think it would be good if the ABC radio started each day with a physical jerks program, like they once did. You'd get out of bed, fling your arms in the 'forwards, upwards, sideways, down' routine for ten minutes, jump in the shower, have your breakfast, and go off to work in a smug glow of self-satisfaction. Not everyone, though. They'd jump out of bed, do the physical jerks, and then jump back into bed. You can't win 'em all.

Place Names

I saw an advertisement for the Pakenham Races in the local paper. Immediately I thought of the course we used to pass in the train, or drove past just this side of Pakenham township when we were going to the station. How wrong could I be! Pakenham Racecourse is now in Tynong. Out there on the Swamp, south of Tynong. But they still call it the Pakenham Racecourse! Seems daft to me. What's wrong with calling it as it is – the Tynong Racecourse? Poor old Tynong. Nothing much happens there for a hundred years, then they get this super-duper racecourse, and they won't even let them name it for Tynong. They're doing this sort of thing all over the place. You know the Bank Place Medical Centre in Drouin? Well, it's in Hopetoun Road. Daft! Completely. It used to be in Bank Place. Some poor geezer might be walking up and down Bank Place all day looking for the Medical Centre, while it's not there at all. He might collapse and have to be flown to hospital. What if we all did that sort of thing? I used to live in Melbourne. I liked the sound of my address there, so I'll keep it now I'm down here, thanks. Look for it in the next phone book.

Playgrounds

We had four young kids down from Melbourne the other day. All boys! By lunchtime we were flagging, but not them. We needed an energy-absorber. So we took them to the playground down the hill. It's not much as playgrounds go, but they thought it was Disneyland. I love it how children like to run! Even when they don't have to. They just set off and run. They ran to the playground, with us trying to keep up. Then they ran from one thing to another – the swings, the slide, the shaky bridge, the climbing frame. And that brute where you have to swing yourself hand to hand across a chain of rings. I call it a brute because I had to carry two eight-year-olds while they did it. There's a super-duper playground up in the new development. Yet there's often no-one at it. Perhaps the kids are developing their computer skills rather than their motor skills. I believe there are a lot of accidents at children's playgrounds. Maybe, but think of what the kids are getting out of these playgrounds, like muscles and confidence and learning to get on with the other kids. I heard of a school once with the motto: 'Mens sana in corpore sano'. A healthy mind in a healthy body. That's pretty neat!

Pounds and Ounces

I wasn't overjoyed when they brought in decimal currency. Then blow me down if they didn't make us all switch over to metres and hectares and kilograms. It'll be driving on the right hand side of the road next. You see, I was good at pounds, shillings and pence. And pounds and ounces. And feet and inches. I learnt it all from the back of those exercise books we had at state school. All the weights and measures were there. How many yards in a furlong, and how many square inches in a square foot. Then they had the tables down the bottom, up to twelve times. 12 x 12 = 144. Then they changed it all and went decimal. Do you know why they did it? There are two possible reasons. (a) to make it easier to do sums. (b) to make us the same as America. Whichever one it was, it didn't work. The kids don't get any better marks for Maths now than they did in the old days, and Britain has stuck with the old system and they get on all right as far as I can see. So I'm looking forward to us going back to the old ways. And to a return of those exercise books with the tables on the back. And if you want to know how many perches in a rood, just ask me. I've kept one of those old books.

Public Art

There's a lot going on in Neerim South. Have you seen the sculpture in the street? You should get out of the car and have a look. And the Neerim Bower – is that what they call it? – the big blue bower bird structure as you're coming in to town. Fair blows your mind. Well, mine, anyway. Some people don't like art, and some people don't like art that's not their kind of art. Public art, especially, comes in for some heavy don't liking. Give it a go, I say. It's funny how a lot of people have to tell everyone if they don't like something – write a letter to the paper or ring the talk-back radio. I suppose they did the same in Ancient Greece, but I'm glad they didn't pull all their statues down or smash their vases. There's a proverb – it's from China – that if you've only got twopence, spend a penny on a rose. (Pennies! Something else those clever Chinese invented). Give art a go, I say. If I don't like it, someone else will. Anyhow, I must say I do like those bollards in Howitt Street on the way out to the hospital in Warragul. And if the Council spends 0.05% of my rates on art works, I won't be writing a letter to the paper to complain about it. Or ringing up the radio.

Queueing Up

They say the English are a nation of queuers. Queuers, not queers. Don't believe it. Warragul beats them hollow. Been to the Post Office lately? You might be out in the street if you're at the end of the queue. I'm not totally against queues, actually. It depends who you're next to. Sometimes you have a lot of fun in the queue. You can build up quite some team spirit. It's more serious at the bank. You get a better look at the tellers there, and you can work out how long you'll have to wait. At the Post Office they put out all these tempting things for sale that you have to walk past, though I haven't ever seen anyone buy even a single one of them. They don't do that at the bank. There's one bank in town that's done away with queues. When you go in, they've got this screen. You work out what you want the bank to do for you and press the button next to it. Then a slip of paper pops out at the bottom with a number on it, like at the deli counter or the RTA. There's a row of comfortable chairs and you sit down on one of them until a mechanical voice calls your number. Then you go and get served. I think they've missed the point. Most of us would rather be in a queue!

Rabbits

Our local cemeteries are for both the living and the dead. I've seen plenty of life in cemeteries. Wild life. In England, some cemeteries are proclaimed nature reserves. Maybe we should do the same. One of my best sightings of wild life was at Corryong, where I saw a six-foot brown snake crawling over a grave slab. It happened to be the Man from Snowy River's grave. But what I'm leading up to is that there's a pretty little family of rabbits in residence at the Gulwarra cemetery in Warragul. Have you seen them? I wonder what they get up to at full moon! There are still quite a few rabbits around the area. We Gippslanders were lucky not to suffer from the rabbit plagues of a hundred years ago. They drove many of our pioneers in other parts off their land. But there were a lot rabbits around these parts when I was a kid. You could earn nice pocket money by trapping (illegal now) and skinning rabbits. Cash for the carcase and cash for the skins. Not to mention ferreting. That was a sport in itself. We'd make ferret boxes out of timber and wire netting. A ferret might kill a rabbit down the burrow and go to sleep. We'd have to dig it out. Not much sport in that!

Radio Stations

Long ago we used to listen to 3UL. They played serials and songs, then on Saturday nights Alf Walton would give the football or cricket results. People would rush home to hear them while they were doing the milking. Vern Haycroft was there, and Max Taylor. Neville Pellitt, too, I think. There were advertisements, as well. They even broadcast the Rotary meetings. There was Radio Market on Saturday mornings, and a Happy Listeners' club. And they did it from the middle of town, in Victoria Street. I heard a story that one of the announcers once put on a record, then went out for a smoke. The door slammed and he was locked out. When the record finished, everyone was listening to the sound of the needle scratching on the record, round and round. Now we've got 3GI from Sale and 774 from Melbourne. I don't know what its proper name is. It used to be 3AR. We can get all the Melbourne stations. You can even choose your own commentator, they've got so many football broadcasts. Then there's ABC FM. And probably more. Not forgetting the new kid on the block, 3BBR, the community station. All volunteers, and they're on air twenty-four hours a day. How do they do it?

Republicanism

Some days I'm a Republican, and some days I'm a Monarchist. It's probably because I'm Irish on my mother's side and English on my Father's side. They used to fight each other. Not my mother and father. The Irish and the English. Other people have very strong views on this. They march in the streets. I think to myself, 'Aren't we a Republic already, except we don't call ourselves that.' The Queen can't do much out here, can she? But then people say it's all symbolic. What are we doing with the Union Jack on our flag, when we come from all over the place, like Vietnam and Sudan and Chile? That's what they say. But the others reckon we got all our laws and our language and our history from Britain, so we shouldn't throw all that out the window. I don't know. It's too hard for me. I did go to see the Queen when she was here, but on the other hand I went to the George Washington memorial when I was in the States. He was the great Republican over there. They actually had a war about it. I wouldn't want to see that here. We seem to find plenty of things to fight about without that. So I'll have to keep sitting on the fence. There seem to be plenty of us up here.

Roundabouts

There's an old joke about all the roundabouts in Warragul. When the streets were being planned, the Shire engineer was in the habit of putting his coffee cup down on the map he was working on. That left a lot of round coffee stains. Someone else picked up the map and thought the stains were roundabouts. So that's where they went. Not true, of course. But those town planners *will* keep fiddling with our streets. One-way in Palmerston Street. One-way in Smith Street. New roundabouts all along Mason Street. Makes me sometimes wish we were a one-street town like Garfield. But still I like Warragul. It's fine if you're walking, but not so good if you're driving a car. So perhaps we could do away with cars. Leave them all outside the CBD (what *does* that stand for?) and turn the shopping area into a huge Mall. We could name it after the Mayor, and change the name every time there's a new one. That would keep us on our toes. To help us get around, the Shire could put in moving stairways – horizontal escalators - like they have at the airports, with a stop at each street corner. I must send the idea to the Shire. Better still, I wonder if there's a vacancy in the town-planning department.

Secondary Schools

Up to the 'fifties, there were only two secondary schools in Warragul, and none in Drouin. The Warragul schools were the High School and the Sisters of Sion College. What a difference now! We've got Marist-Sion, St Paul's, and the Regional College in Warragul, and the Secondary College and Chairo in Drouin. In my day, nearly all the kids dropped out of school before Year 12. Now, it's the other way round. Nearly all stay on to the end of school. I wonder what it's like being in Year 12 nowadays. We were sure of a job or a university place. These days, a lot of young people are unemployed, and you have to pay hefty fees to go to university. They say we've come a long way in the last half-century, but I'm not so sure. There are all these technological advances, but young people today face a hard future. More than we did. So where's the gain? Maybe I'm being pessimistic. The young folk seem pretty cheerful, most of them. I guess they're more adaptable than we were. And life can still be sweet, especially if your footy team's winning, you're getting three meals a day, and you've got some mates. Come to think about it, they're the same things we cared most about, too.

Shopping

Now what is it she wants? I'm pacing the aisles looking at the shelves trying to remember what my wife asked me to buy. I can remember two of the three - milk and bread – but I know there was a third. A woman looks at me and I realise I'm muttering to myself, 'Now what is it she wants me to get?' So I tell her. She laughs, but can't help. 'You'll be in trouble,' she says. I often ask women in the supermarket if I can't find something on my list. They always help, especially when I put on my poor helpless male act. Sometimes they take me right to the spot. In some stores they have a shopping guide. It's a list of everything they sell and which aisle it's in. But I can never find the shopping guide, so that's no help. So there I am, in the check-out queue with my bread and milk, still trying to remember. Then I see the batteries and chocolates and other things they want you to buy on impulse. (A lot of people can't resist a good battery, you know.) Throat tablets! That's it. That's the third thing. So I'm looking for them while I'm moving along in the queue. I get to the check-out, so that does it. I give up. 'Couldn't find the throat tablets,' I say to my wife.

Tattoos

I watched the football on the TV. They had all these Maoris and Hawaiians playing. Tattoos all over them! Then I went down the street and it was the same. There are tattoo shops, these days, alongside the coffee shops and the hairdressers. They're mostly young folk who get tattoos. They're mostly older folk who have them removed. In New Zealand, the tattooist decides which tattoo you have, not the customer. I reckon if they had that rule here, we wouldn't see so many tattoos. I know a woman who had a new tattoo every time she moved house. Each one stood for the new place. With all these tattoos, there could be some trouble down the track. Especially when you see on some young fellow's arm, 'I love you Susie'. What if Susie breaks it off? The next girl mightn't be too happy. Never get a tattoo done overseas. I heard about a bloke visiting China who asked for a tattoo of 'Happiness' in Chinese. But the tattoo man did an advertisement for his shop instead. The young bloke never knew. I don't want you to think I'm against tattoos. We always have fashions. Let the young people follow their fashion, I say. Hang on a minute. What's that? My grandson wants a tattoo? Help!

The Dentist

I've been going to the dentist for a long time. It started when I was in state school, and the school dentist came round every year. We were called out two at a time to face the music. Later on, another dentist came round to the local hall on Saturdays, and he'd take out our teeth in the Supper Room. That's all he did – take out teeth, nothing else. Everyone lost their teeth, and got false ones. Have you seen those old photos of the football teams? With their mouths all pinched in? They've all got their teeth out. They'd take them out before the match, put them in their coat pockets, and run on to the field. No mouth guards then. When teeth care got better, they didn't need coat pockets any more, and that's why coats went out of fashion. That's what I reckon. I was at the dentist's not long ago. He said I needed a filling, a big one. 'Do you have a needle for a filling,' he said. 'Do other people have needles?' I asked. 'Some do, some don't,' he said back. So, acting the tough guy, I said, 'Go ahead, Alfonso.' And he did. Didn't hurt a bit. The filling came out a few weeks later, and I went back. He told me I'd have to have the tooth out. 'Do you have a needle for an extraction?' he asked.

The Highway

Some of the old folk out Neerim way tell me their grandparents used to walk from Melbourne and even further to take up their selections, and they carried their tools with them. They often take weeks to do it. Now we whizz down the highway in an hour or two in our sleek cars. I did it just the other day. I'm sure it's shorter now we have kilometres instead of miles. Ten kilometres is nothing, but ten miles! That took an age. And what happened to all the mileposts? They had them one every mile. I wish I had one now. You don't see any kilometre posts. I suppose they'd run out of money putting them in and looking after them all. By the way, I see they've fixed up that Sand Road intersection on the highway at Longwarry. Now it's a hundred kilometres an hour instead of eighty. Wow! That will put house prices up in Drouin. One minute closer to town. And there's so much traffic. When I was a kid we used to go to the highway and count the cars. We'd say to each other, I can hear one coming. And sure enough one would come along within a minute or two. I don't think Health and Safety would let us do that now. And we'd need a clicker to count them anyway.

The Library

Do you remember when we weren't allowed to talk in the library? If we did, we got dirty looks from the old ladies. They were the chief customers in those days. Now you can talk as loud as you like, and it's the librarians who talk the loudest. It's more like a meeting place than a library. Like Everybody's Club – without the joining fees. The kids romp around; people read them stories out loud. They sometimes have meetings as if it was a public hall. Nobody minds. You can order a book from another library and they'll get it for you. They'll sometimes buy a book just for you if they haven't got it anywhere. They've got large print books if you can't see too well, and books on tape if you can't see at all. If your paper isn't delivered, just duck down to the library. They've got it there. If you want to find out if they've got a book, you just look it up on their computer. And there are other computers to use for whatever you want, no questions asked. If you want something photocopied, hey presto, you do it there. And they've got thousands of books. Everybody's Club? More like a Club, Workshop, and Learning Centre, all in one. And somewhere to keep out of the rain.

The Old Order Changeth

So Robert Murphy has retired. The Western Suburbs of Melbourne are heavy with grief, and Warragul more so. Bob Murphy's our own boy. A Warragul boy. It's the way of the world. People – or ideas or even nations – grow strong, they reach their peak, they subside, and they pass away. Tennyson – Alfred, Lord Tennyson, remember? – wrote about the death of King Arthur, he of the Round Table. King Arthur floated out on the evening tide saying, 'The old order changeth, yielding place to new.' Great last words! There were others to take up King Arthur's work, however. Similarly, there will be others to take up Bob Murphy's work (though they won't be so perfectly balanced, nor kick so well, nor write like him in the 'Age'). They're rare, these fluid, artistic, poetic, players. Neil Harvey did it for cricket. Bob Murphy did it for football, and so did Thorold Merrett and Robert Flower and Michael Long. We can't hang on to them. The forest giant crashes, but already the saplings are growing up to take its place. But we won't have Bob Murphy himself. Not out on the ground. He will still be Bob Murphy, however, and football will still be football. Maybe!

The A2 986

There are some things that will just never go away. Like steam trains. All huff and puff, grit and grime, smells and smoke. I thought we'd had enough of them. Replaced them with smart, efficient, environmentally-friendly diesels that glide glibly down the well-oiled tracks. But no. It seems I'm wrong. Everybody hankers after the old steam monsters. Take that A2 986 that used to be in the park in Warragul, a rusty old dinosaur quietly fading away to obscurity. They take it to Melbourne, work on it for thirty years, and bring it back in all its old glory. Then five thousand people turn out to see it, as though there was nothing else to do on a Saturday morning. Well, like an unwelcome wedding guest, I couldn't stay away. Do you know, it fair brought tears to my eyes. I was suddenly living again in those heady days when, as a boy, I'd ride this wild horse to Melbourne, head out the window, hearing again the workmen's cries of 'Paper! Paper!' from beside the line, wanting us to toss them out an 'Argus' or a 'Sun'. Ah, here's Dandenong ... now Caulfield ... there's the Yarra River ... the Bryant and May chimney... and, at last, Flinders Street. This is life!

Tomatoes

I'm like most people. I'm good at some things and not good at other things. And some things I'm half good at. One of those is gardening. Half what I sow comes up. I'm better where you buy a plant and put it in the ground, like tomatoes, but even there I have my disappointments. We had only one tomato this year. Quite a few plants, but only one tomato. Tom Thumbs and Green Thumbs don't go together in our household. Our lone tomato grew stoutly for some weeks. It was an inch and a half across. We admired it and spoke encouragingly to it. This morning we found it mortally wounded. Some wriggling creature, or was it a bird – or perhaps some jealous neighbour had wreaked irrecoverable injury under the cover of darkness. While we slept in our sweet innocence, dark deeds were being perpetrated outside our window. What to do now? We can't eat it. It might give us psittacosis or worms. The only thing is to arrange a decent burial in the compost bin. From dust you came and unto dust you shall return. Or, as Shakespeare said, 'Fear no more the heat of the sun, nor the furious winter's rages; thou thy worldly task hast done; home art gone and ta'en thy wages.'

Utopia

All the talk a while ago was about Utopia. I couldn't get the hang of it at first. Utopia, to my mind, was a book by Thomas More about a place of perfection. Like heaven on earth. Samuel Butler wrote another one like that. His place of perfection was called Erewhon, and you get the drift of what he thought about it when you turn the letters round backwards. Isn't there supposed to be another place called Shangri-La hidden away in the Himalayas? Anyway, it turns out that this Utopia was a place to take your pets when you go away for a holiday, and the Council wanted to turn it into the local pound. There was the dickens of a row about it. I thought there was a simple solution. Turn our street into the pound. Block off each end and let the animals go free, like they do now. A few more would hardly be noticed. The animals would love it. Free to fight all day. The residents could be issued with passes to get in and out, and the fees could be used to pay a man to open and close the gates, like they used to do on the railway line. That way, they'd please everyone – dogs, cats, the Council. And the people who live here wouldn't notice the difference. Sounds like a Utopian solution to me.

Vision Australia

There are some units not far from my place. I was walking past them when I saw a youngish chap standing outside. I said gooday, then I noticed he had a white cane. It turned out he was blind. We got talking. He was waiting for a friend to pick him up and take him to Vision Australia in Albert Street in Warragul. He was telling me all about it. They do a whole lot of things. A whole lot of people work there as volunteers. There are different activities they put on. Sometimes they go on outings. They can't fix your sight, but they help you with all sorts of things to make it easier to live with blindness or low vision. They can arrange to fit out your house with devices to help you. All sorts of things. I was amazed. They've even got a radio station there, where they read the newspapers over the air, and things like that. Everyone can listen in. 93.5 FM, he told me. The best thing is everyone has a whale of a time. We don't think of these things most of the time, but we've got tucked away there a place that's changing the lives of a heap of people. It makes me feel it wouldn't be too bad to be blind after all. And, maybe I could volunteer and be part of it all. There's a thought!

Walking in the Street

A lot of good things happen in the street. Especially our street. Whenever I've got nothing to do, I go and see what's happening out there. People walk past our house a lot. I stand at the gate and watch them. The best time is early in the morning. You get all kinds then – women taking dogs, dogs taking women, older folk (sometimes these come in pairs), young men with babies on their backs, like eskimos, and every now and then a group of young women with water bottles in their hands. I've never asked these people why they walk. It must be something to do with the uncertainties of life. Ants do the same – go round in circles when something goes wrong. It's the same in Drouin, I believe, this walking in streets, and it's spreading to Neerim South and other places. I confess that I sometimes go and walk in the streets myself. I say hello to people I meet. The old ones answer. In fact they often stop and talk, especially if they're going up-hill. The young ones mostly don't say anything. Perhaps they think I wouldn't be interested in them. The generational divide! You should try this new walking game. It's good for you. My neck muscles are a lot stronger from nodding to people.

Walking Track

They put in this walking track between Drouin and Warragul. The Two Towns Trail they call it. Spent millions on it. But a lot of people use it. I see them out of the car window. You see people riding bikes too. I did it once. It's very steep in places. I always think it's a shame that they flatten out the road for cars, which don't need it, while the walkers and bike-riders, who do need it, have to go up all the hills. The worst part is where the track is close to the main road, and you get the noise of trucks and cars in your ear. But it's a lot more peaceful when you get away from the road. I see a lot of people who are getting near Warragul, and I wonder if they've walked the whole way from Drouin or whether they've walked out from Warragul, turned round, and come back. You're allowed to do that, I think. They should have a certificate you get if you've walked the whole way, like they do with charity walks and fun runs and things like that. The time I rode along there, my bike broke down, and blow-me-down if a guy on a motor scooter – one of those gophers, I think they call them – didn't come along and fix it for me. That's the fellowship of the road for you.

We're Multicultural

When you stop to think about it, we're a pretty multicultural crowd in this part of Gippsland. Some of us live in towns with aboriginal names, like Neerim and Bunyip and Warragul. But Drouin's named after a Frenchman, Catani after an Italian, Labertouche after another Frenchman, Strzelecki after a Pole. And if you look a bit further, Churchill gets its name from some guy in Britain. Have you ever been to Churchill? They've got this huge pillar stuck up in the middle of the town. It's supposed to look like Churchill's cigar. You see people from other countries walking round in our streets all the time. I should ask them where they come from. I went to China once. The people there were very friendly, and they often came and spoke to me. That's what we should do here, except we're all too Anglo-Saxon and reserved. But we mean well. There's a mob here in Warragul and roundabout who get together and talk peace and things like that. They've got these peace poles, they call them, and they put them up in different places. And they write things on these poles, like, 'May peace prevail on earth'. I suppose it does some good. What did the song say? The world needs love?

Winning Tatts

I sometimes think what I'd do if I won Tattslotto. Not the little Saturday one, but one of the big weekday ones. Twenty-five million. Fifty million. I'm mostly in bed when I think these thoughts. No one must know, I'd won. I suppose my wife would have to, but I'm not sure. I'd be the person who gave anonymously to all the local causes. Very generously! I'd have to have someone who was in on the secret to give out the money. Everybody would want to know who was doing it. I'd be laughing up my sleeve when people were talking about it. I might fix some of the local problems. Lend the Council ten million interest free to build a car park in Warragul, another ten million for Drouin for a community hub on that land in the main street, five million for Hillview, and something for the Neerim South Hospital. Maybe I could give it all to cancer research. Or send it to Oxfam or Doctors without Borders. Nothing for myself. Still the same old clothes. Same house. Maybe I'd get the car fixed up. No-one would notice that. And perhaps the kids could have a bit, though I wouldn't want to spoil them. It's about then I go to sleep. I must see about getting a ticket. Now, how do you do that?

Yarragon

Yarragon's the place that everyone takes their visitors to. When you get there you meet all your friends who are taking their visitors there also. So does anyone actually live there? Or is just a town of visitors? No, there are people who live in Yarragon. I know two of them. They say it's a really daggy place. You can walk to the shops. It's got a market once a month. The shops are off the main road. And there's an art gallery in the railway station. Now, that's cute. Though you've got other art galleries if you don't fancy that one. I don't know if they made them do it, but most of the shops are the same yellowy-brown colour, so when you think of Yarragon, you've got a colour pattern in your head. There aren't too many places like that. There's a football team in Yarragon, and I look up their result each week. It's not happy reading. But Yarragon will rise from the ashes. And winning isn't everything! I don't know where Yarragon got its name, but I looked up the internet, and there's no other town called Yarragon on the face of the earth. Now that's really something. You can tell the locals from the newcomers by the way they pronounce Yarragon. Watch that last syllable.

Last Words

I feel like Michelangelo must have felt when he finished the ceiling of the Sistine Chapel. He laid down his brush and I've laid down my pen. Thanks for being with me over these eighty pages. We're full of surprises, we West Gippslanders. Behind our front doors you'll find an amazing range of people, all contributing mightily to society – university lecturers, foreign aid workers, sports champions, town planners, international adventurers, anaesthetists, and aged pensioners, Council workers, florists, and motor apprentices. All tagged with the same brush. We come from Drouin. We come from Warragul. We're West Gippslanders. And we make it what it is. Now, like Bob Murphy, I hang up my boots. Time to have a rest. That reminds me of my favourite cemetery plaque. It's in the Drouin Cemetery and it marks the grave of Keith Forbes, who played football in Melbourne, and later coached Drouin. It says, simply, *'Resting in the forward pocket'*. That's what I'll be doing for a while. Resting in the forward pocket. But watch out! I'll still be casting my eye over the local scene, and who knows, you might finish up in a second edition if you're not careful.

www.ingramcontent.com/pod-product-compliance
Lightning Source LLC
Chambersburg PA
CBHW021026120726
47905CB00009B/3193